Essential Oils for Infants

A comprehensive guide on how to harness the power of nature's essences for your infant's health, vitality, and longevity.

Dr. Amalie Kleist

Table of Contents

DISCLAIMER

This content is not meant to offer medical advice or replace advice or treatment from a personal physician. It is recommended that you get advice from your doctors or trained health specialists for any specific health inquiries you may have. Readers or followers of this instructional resource are responsible for any potential health effects.

Introduction

In the calm of infancy, there is a world of exquisite wonder, where each coo and sigh is a symphony of life unfolding. Our roles as parents, guardians, and caretakers overwhelm us with an unending urge to care for and safeguard these priceless beings.

However, even with the benefits of being a parent, we frequently face the difficulties that come with raising an infant—the gentle screams of pain, the small sniffles of congestion, and the heart-wrenching sleepless nights. In these times of vulnerability, we seek comfort not only in treatments but also in kind, natural companions for our children.

Discover the world of essential oils: a distillation of the purest essences found in nature, packed into little vials that hold immense therapeutic potential. As an enthusiastic and committed supporter of holistic wellness, Dr. Amalie Kleist extends an invitation to explore the world of "Essential Oils for Infants."

On these pages, Dr. Kleist combines her knowledge of holistic medicine with her great respect for plant extracts' therapeutic benefits. She reveals a vast array of treatments designed especially for the requirements of infants, drawing on both contemporary scientific research and millennia of traditional wisdom. She walks parents and other caregivers through the art and science of utilizing essential oils to enhance their children's wellbeing with a mild touch and a kind heart.

In "Essential Oils for Infants," Dr. Kleist offers a comprehensive approach to infant care that respects the body's inherent intelligence and Mother Nature's protective embrace, in addition to a list of remedies. By providing advice on dilution, application methods, and safety precautions, she enables readers to safely and effectively harness the therapeutic potential of essential oils. From the calming scents of lavender to the reassuring warmth of chamomile, every chapter resonates with Dr. Kleist's love of holistic medicine and her steadfast dedication to the wellbeing of infants. She tackles common ailments like colic, discomfort associated with teething, and respiratory problems with compassion and clarity, providing natural remedies that harmonize with the cycles of the natural world. May this path of discovery lead you to uncover moments of connection rather than merely remedies—moments when the soft touch of essential oils becomes a sweet expression of love, a whisper of comfort in your children's ears.

More than just a book, "Essential Oils for Infants" is a monument to the healing power of the natural world and a beacon of hope for all babies seeking holistic well-being.

Chapter One

What are essential oils?

Essential oils are concentrated liquids derived from plants. They capture the "essence" of the plant's fragrance and flavor. Usually, cold pressing or distillation extract these oils. The natural fragrant chemicals present in plants give these oils their distinctive fragrance.

A variety of civilizations have used essential oils for their therapeutic and medical benefits since ancient times. Aromatherapy frequently utilizes essential oils, inhaling their scent to promote calmness and relaxation or alleviate tension and anxiety. Furthermore, some essential oils, when applied topically or consumed, are believed to have antimicrobial, anti-inflammatory, or other health-promoting qualities; however, it's crucial to use them safely and consult a healthcare provider if you have any questions or concerns about any specific medical conditions.

What is the mechanism by which essential oils work?

Aromatherapy, which involves inhaling essential oils using a variety of techniques, is the most popular application for them.

It is not recommended to ingest essential oils. Your body might react to the compounds in essential oils in a number of ways. Applying topically absorbs a certain amount of plant compounds.

Certain application techniques, such as applying heat to different parts of the body, may enhance absorption. However, research in this field remains limited.

Inhaling the fragrances of essential oils can activate certain parts of your limbic system, a brain region involved in emotions, behavior, smell perception, and long-term memory. It's interesting to note that memory formation largely involves the limbic system. This helps partially explain why odors that are familiar to you might evoke feelings or memories. In addition, the limbic system regulates a number of unconscious physiological processes, including blood pressure, heart rate, and respiration. Because of this, some individuals assert that essential oils have a physical impact on your body. However, research has not yet proven this.

Understanding essential oils for infants

Safety is the most important factor when it comes to using essential oils on infants. The following are important safety measures and rules for dilution to keep in mind:

Safety precautions:

- Before applying essential oils on or near infants, always get advice from a physician or other licensed healthcare provider.

- Infants younger than three months old should use essential oils with caution; in fact, some experts advise against using them at all during this time.

- To avoid accidentally ingesting essential oils or coming into contact with delicate tissues like the eyes and mucous membranes, keep them out of children's reach.

- Avoid putting undiluted essential oils straight on an infant's skin. Always dilute essential oils with a carrier oil before using them.

- When applying essential oils to infants, be aware of any indications of sensitivity or allergic reactions. Should any negative reactions arise, stop using the product right away and consult a doctor.

Dilution Guidelines:

- Generally, experts recommend using a significantly lower dilution ratio for infants compared to adults. Generally speaking, a safe starting point is between 0.1% and 0.25% dilution, or 1 to 2 drops of essential oil for every ounce (30 ml) of carrier oil.

- Sweet almond oil, coconut oil, jojoba oil, or olive oil are good carrier oils to dilute essential oils for infants. Using these carrier oils reduces the risk of skin irritation.

- Infants' sensitive respiratory systems may be

overstimulated by the strong aroma of essential oils, so avoid putting them in or close to their mouths, noses, or faces.

- Use small amounts of essential oil, and make sure there is enough ventilation when using an essential oil diffuser near a baby. Keep the diffuser in a well-ventilated place and use it occasionally rather than constantly.

Pure essential oils require dilution with a carrier oil or cream when applied topically due to their high concentration. Even after dilution, they may irritate the skin and cause sun sensitivity. With every fresh oil application, we advise doing a patch test on your baby's arms or legs and protecting them from the sun for the following 24 hours or so.

How a Patch Test Is Performed

✓ A diluted essential oil should be applied to a baby's

17

arm or leg, no larger than a dime.

✓ Be patient and wait 24 hours to see what happens.

✓ If you have a response like redness, swelling, or pain, stop using it.

✓ It's probably okay to continue applying the essential oil if there is no reaction.

All things considered, the key to utilizing essential oils with infants is moderation and caution. Prioritizing safety is essential, and you should speak with medical specialists to get advice suited to your child's unique needs and situation.

Chapter Two

15 Essential oils safe for infants: benefits, usage tips and precautions

Safety should always come first when choosing essential oils for use with infants. Choose oils that are mild and well-tolerated by young children. Experts generally consider the following list of essential oils, along with information on their safe use and benefits, to be suitable for infants:

Lavender Oil

Benefits: Lavender oil has become known for being calming and soothing, which helps aid in sleep and relaxation.

Usage Tips: Dilute 1-2 drops of lavender oil in a carrier oil and use it for infant massage before bedtime. To make the infant's room feel peaceful, you may also put a few drops in a diffuser.

Precautions: Make sure you dilute the product properly, and stop using it if you experience any irritation or allergic reactions

Chamomile Oil (Roman)

Benefits: Roman chamomile oil has mild sedative qualities and is frequently used to help babies feel more relaxed and relieved from gastrointestinal distress.

Usage Tips: For a relaxing bath, add a few drops to bath water, or dilute 1-2 drops in carrier oil and massage it into your baby.

Precautions: Always dilute thoroughly and don't use for extended periods of time, as chamomile allergies may occur in certain infants.

Frankincense Oil

Benefits: Frankincense oil has a grounding scent and is believed to strengthen the immune system. It may also encourage calmness and a sense of relaxation.

Usage Tips: Dilute 1-2 drops of frankincense oil in a carrier oil and use it for gentle massage, or diffuse it in the nursery to create a peaceful environment.

Precautions: Use caution when using, and stop using immediately if any negative side effects appear.

Dill Oil

Benefits: Infants with digestive issues like gas and colic often benefit from the use of dill oil.

Usage Tips: Dilute 1-2 drops of dill oil in a carrier oil

and lightly massage the baby's abdomen in a clockwise direction to help relieve gas.

Precautions: Always dilute properly, avoiding getting into the eyes or mucous membranes.

Mandarin Oil

Benefits: The pleasant, uplifting scent of mandarin oil helps elevate mood and encourage rest.

Usage Tips: Dilute 1-2 drops of mandarin oil in a carrier oil and use it for a gentle massage, or add a few drops to a diffuser to create a cheerful atmosphere.

Precautions: Ensure proper dilution and avoid prolonged exposure to sunlight after topical application, as mandarin oil can cause photosensitivity.

Cedarwood Oil

Benefits: It promotes respiratory health and is calming. The body benefits greatly from cedarwood oil, which enhances general wellbeing.

Usage Tips: Dilute 1-2 drops of mandarin oil in a carrier oil and massage it gently.

Precaution: It may cause skin irritation in some people.

Grapeseed Oil

Benefits: It is a mild moisturizer and works well as a carrier oil.

Usage Tips: Before applying essential oils topically, dilute them in grapeseed oil.

Precautions: Make sure it's organic and food-grade.

Rose Oil

Benefits: It promotes emotional wellbeing and it calms the body and mind with its delicate flowery aroma. Additionally, it calms a baby's restlessness and hydrates the skin.

Usage Tips: highly diluted in a carrier oil for massage or added to a diffuser.

Precaution: Because of its extreme potency, use it with expert advice and caution.

Sweet Orange Oil

Benefits: It is uplifting and may also aid digestion.

Usage Tips: Add to a diffuser or dilute in carrier oil for massaging. Diffusing a few drops in the bedroom will cheer up a baby.

Precautions: Phototoxic, so avoid direct sunlight after use on skin.

Lemon Oil

Benefits: Vibrant and tangy lemon oil improves mood. Diffusing it after nap time is a good idea.

Usage Tips: Apply a few drops of essential oil diffuser or gently massage the oil into the baby's skin, beginning with the legs.

Precaution: Avoid diffusing essential oils for infants for more than an hour.

Petitgrain Oil

Benefits: Petitgrain oil is a great way to moisturize dry skin. Both adults and newborns experience mood elevation from its floral and woodsy smell.

Usage Tips: Apply 1-2 drops of essential oil diffuser or gently massage the oil into the baby's skin, beginning with the legs.

Precaution: Avoid diffusing essential oils for infants for more than an hour.

Grapefruit Oil

Benefits: Prevent musty odors in the nursery. With a tangy scent that awakens the senses, grapefruit oil purifies and refreshes the atmosphere.

Usage Tips: Apply 1-2 drops of essential oil diffuser or gently massage the oil into the baby's skin, beginning with the legs.

Precaution: Avoid diffusing essential oils for infants for more than an hour.

Tangerine oil

Benefits: You can use tangerine oil to create a calming atmosphere for both parents and babies.

Usage Tips: Apply 1-2 drops of essential oil diffuser or gently massage the oil into the baby's skin, beginning with the legs.

Precaution: Avoid diffusing essential oils for infants for more than an hour.

Bergamot Oil

Benefits: Bergamot oil's sweet, citrus, and tangy smell offers elevating effects that help with depressed moods. It also soothes the mind.

Usage Tips: Apply 1-2 drops of essential oil diffuser or gently massage the oil into the baby's skin, beginning with the legs.

Precaution: Avoid diffusing essential oils for infants for more than an hour.

Ylang Ylang oil

Benefits: Ylang ylang oil is exotic and flowery, calming moods and preparing your kids for naps.

Usage Tips: Apply 1-2 drops of essential oil diffuser or gently massage the oil into the baby's skin, beginning with the legs.

Precaution: Avoid diffusing essential oils for infants for more than an hour.

Moderation, appropriate dilution, and safety should always come first when using essential oils with infants. Before incorporating essential oils into your baby's routine, it is imperative that you speak with a physician or other experienced healthcare provider. This is especially important if your baby has any underlying medical issues or sensitivities. Furthermore, closely monitor your infant's response to essential oils and cease their use if any adverse effects manifest.

Chapter Three

18 Blends of essential oils and recipes for infants

We provide the following recipes and essential oil blends, along with instructions on how to prepare and use them.

Calm Sleep Blend

Ingredients: lavender oil, Roman chamomile oil, and vetiver oil.

Preparation: In a dark glass bottle, combine 3 drops of lavender oil, 2 drops of Roman chamomile oil, and 1 drop of vetiver oil.

Usage: To encourage deep and peaceful sleep, diffuse a few drops of the blend in the bedroom before going to bed.

Calm Baby Blend

Ingredients: Mandarin oil, Frankincense oil, lavender oil.

Preparation: Combine 2 drops of Mandarin oil, 1 drop of Frankincense oil, and 1 drop of Lavender oil in a dark glass bottle.

Usage: To soothe and relax the infant, dilute 1-2 drops of the combination in carrier oil and massage onto their back and chest.

Gentle Belly Relief Blend

Ingredients: cardamom oil, ginger oil, and peppermint oil.

Preparation: In a dark glass bottle, combine 1 drop cardamom oil, 1 drop ginger oil, and 1 drop peppermint oil.

Usage: To help with digestion, dilute 1 drop of the blend in a teaspoon of carrier oil and gently massage the baby's stomach in a clockwise direction.

Blend to soothe and improve skin

Ingredients: chamomile oil, lavender oil, and coconut oil.

Preparation: Mix 2 drops of chamomile oil and 2 drops of lavender oil into 1 tablespoon of melted coconut oil.

Usage: For soothing comfort, apply just a little of the blend to the baby's skin in areas of irritation or diaper rash.

Comforting and Calming Blend

Ingredients: Bergamot oil, Cedar wood oil, and

Sandalwood oil.

Preparation: Combine 2 drops of Bergamot oil, 1 drop of cedarwood oil, and 1 drop of Sandalwood oil in a dark glass bottle.

Usage: Dilute and apply to pulse points for relaxation, or diffuse the blend around the space to produce a soothing mood.

Congestion Relief Blend for Babies

Ingredients: lemon oil, tea tree oil, and eucalyptus oil.

Preparation: In a dark glass bottle, combine 1 drop each of eucalyptus oil, tea tree oil, and lemon oil.

Usage: Apply a diluted mixture to the chest and back for respiratory comfort, or diffuse it throughout the room to help remove congestion.

Joyful Infant Blend

Ingredients: sweet orange oil, geranium oil, and ylang ylang oil.

Preparation: In a dark glass bottle, combine 2 drops of sweet orange oil, 1 drop of geranium oil, and 1 drop of ylang ylang oil.

Usage: To improve the baby's mood and create a joyful environment, diffuse the blend.

Blend for growth and development

Ingredients: rosemary oil, frankincense oil, and lavender oil.

Preparation: Combine 2 drops of rosemary oil, 1 drop of frankincense oil, and 1 drop of lavender oil in a dark glass bottle.

Usage: To encourage healthy growth and development, massage a diluted combination over the baby's feet or diffuse the blend during playtime.

Teething Pain Relief Mix

Ingredients: clove oil, lavender oil, and coconut oil.

Preparation: Combine 1 drop of clove oil, 2 drops of lavender oil, and 1 tablespoon of melted coconut oil. *Usage:* To help relieve teething discomfort, gently massage a tiny amount of the blend onto the baby's gums.

Blend for a Calm Bedtime

Ingredients: Bergamot oil, lavender oil, and cedarwood oil.

Preparation: In a dark glass bottle, combine 2 drops of Bergamot oil, 2 drops of lavender oil, and 1 drop of

Cedarwood oil.

Usage: To create a relaxing atmosphere for the bedtime routine, diffuse the blend in the bedroom.

Tranquil Bath Mix

Ingredients: jojoba oil, lavender oil, and chamomile oil.

Preparation: Combine 2 drops of chamomile oil, 3 drops of lavender oil, and 1 tablespoon of jojoba oil.

Usage: To give your infant a relaxing and peaceful bath, blend the mixture into the water.

Immune Boost Blend

Ingredients: lemon oil, tea tree oil, and thyme oil.

Preparation: In a dark glass bottle, combine 2 drops lemon oil, 1 drop tea tree oil, and 1 drop thyme oil.

Usage: During the cold and flu season, diffuse the blend across the baby's room to strengthen their immune system.

Invigorating Playtime Blend

Ingredients: sweet orange oil, peppermint oil, and rosemary oil.

Preparation: Combine 2 drops of sweet orange oil, 1 drop of peppermint oil, and 1 drop of rosemary oil in a dark glass bottle.

Usage: To stimulate the senses and encourage attentiveness during playtime, diffuse the blend.

Energizing Citrus Mix

Ingredients: lemon oil, grapefruit oil, and bergamot oil.

Preparation: In a dark glass bottle, blend together 2

drops lemon oil, 1 drop grapefruit oil, and 1 drop bergamot oil.

Usage: To create a bright and cheery ambiance in the baby's room, diffuse the mix.

Wellness Baby Massage Blend

Ingredients: lavender oil, chamomile oil, and sweet almond oil.

Preparation: Mix 1 tablespoon of sweet almond oil with 1 drop each of chamomile and lavender oils.

Usage: For mild baby massages to promote bonding, relaxation, and skin hydration.

Blend for a Cozy Cuddle

Ingredients: rose, lavender, and sandalwood oils.

Preparation: Combine 2 drops of lavender oil, 1 drop of

rose oil, and 1 drop of sandalwood oil in a dark glass bottle.

Usage: Apply a gentle massage to the infant's back to promote comfort and relaxation during cuddle time.

Mild Digestive Mixture

Ingredients: fennel oil, ginger oil, and peppermint oil.

Preparation: In a dark glass bottle, combine 1 drop ginger oil, 1 drop peppermint oil, and 1 drop fennel oil.

Usage: To relieve digestive problems in babies, dilute with carrier oil and massage onto the baby's tummy.

Calendula Blend for Calmness

Ingredients: calendula oil, lavender oil, and coconut oil.

Preparation: Combine 2 drops of calendula and 2 drops of lavender oil with 1 tablespoon of heated coconut oil.

Usage: Apply to dry or irritated skin to provide hydration and calming comfort.

It is imperative to dilute essential oils appropriately before applying them to infants and to stop using them if any negative responses develop.

Additionally, it is crucial to remember to store these mixtures in dark glass containers, shielded from direct sunlight and high temperatures, in order to maintain their effectiveness. Prior to applying essential oils to or near infants, it is advisable to seek guidance from a healthcare expert.

Chapter Four

Essential oil application methods for infants: benefits and risks

It is vital to examine the potential advantages and hazards of different techniques for applying essential oils to infants. Below is a summary of some popular application techniques, along with the benefits and risks of each:

Diffusion

Using a diffuser is one of the safest methods to introduce essential oils to infants. Place a water-filled diffuser in the infant's room and add a few drops of a baby-safe essential oil to it. Ensure the space has adequate ventilation and only occasionally turn on the diffuser to prevent overexposure.

- ***Benefits:*** By creating a nice aroma in the space, essential oils can help soothe and elevate the moods of both caregivers and newborns. Certain essential oils, like lavender, chamomile, and mandarin, have a reputation for being calming, which makes them useful for helping babies fall asleep and become less fussy.

- ***Risks:*** While diffusion is generally considered safe, it's important to use a low dilution and ensure adequate ventilation to prevent overexposure. Keep a close watch on your infant's reactions, as some may be sensitive to certain essential oils or find powerful scents overwhelming.

Diluted Massage

Babies can benefit from a mild massage using essential oils diluted in a carrier oil. Add one to two drops of essential oil to each ounce of baby-safe carrier oil, such as coconut, almond, or jojoba oil. Avoid sensitive areas, such as the face, and instead massage the diluted oil onto the bottoms of the baby's feet or onto their back.

- *Benefits:* Diluted essential oils applied gently to the infant can ease discomfort from teething or gas, induce relaxation, and strengthen the link between caregiver and child. Some oils, such as mild citrus oils or chamomile, can also help maintain healthy skin.

- *Risks:* Using oils not intended for babies or incorrectly diluting them can irritate their skin or trigger allergic reactions. Avoid delicate areas like the face; always do a patch test; and start with a low dilution ratio. Furthermore, excessive pressure or frequent use of oils during massages may cause pain in babies.

Aromatherapy Inhalation

Another safe technique is to put a cotton ball or piece of tissue near the baby's crib or changing table, then add a drop of a baby-friendly essential oil to it. This lets the baby take a gentle sniff of the scent. To avoid ingesting it or skin contact, make sure the essential oil is out of the infant's reach.

- *Benefits:* Inhaling pleasant smells from essential oils can relax newborns, relieve congestion, and enhance respiratory health. Tea tree or eucalyptus oil vapors, for instance, can aid in clearing nasal passages.

- *Risks:* Strong scents or menthol-rich oils, such as those of peppermint or eucalyptus, can be too strong for babies, irritating their respiratory systems or making breathing difficult. To prevent overexposure, always use mild oils and make sure there is enough ventilation.

Hydrosols

Often referred to as floral waters, hydrosols are kinder substitutes for essential oils and may be safer to use on young children. Steam-distilled plants create them, incorporating water-soluble ingredients and minute amounts of essential oil. You can dilute hydrosols with water or softly spray them into the air for an enhanced aromatic experience.

- *Benefits:* Hydrosols might be safer to use on young children and are a milder substitute for essential oils. Though in a softer state, they still have some of the plant's medicinal qualities. You can dilute and mist hydrosols lightly to create a mildly scented bath experience.

- *Risks:* Despite the general perception of hydrosols as harmless, some newborns may experience sensitivities due to certain plant extracts. It's critical to keep an eye out for any indications of irritation or discomfort, and to stop using the product if necessary.

Room Sprays

Use a spray bottle to sprinkle the air in the baby's room after diluting essential oils that are suitable for babies with water. Make sure the area has enough airflow, and keep the spray from getting on the baby's skin or blankets.

- *Benefits:* Natural room sprays can contribute to a calming atmosphere for babies by adding a light scent to the surrounding air. They can also aid in eliminating offensive smells and enhancing cleanliness.

- *Risks:* Certain commercial room sprays might include chemicals or artificial aromas that are harmful to young children. When choosing a spray, always go for natural, baby-safe components and refrain from sprinkling the baby's skin or sheets directly.

When applied correctly, essential oils can assist babies, but moderation and safety must always come first. Prior to using essential oils on newborns, always get medical advice, conduct patch tests, and keep a close eye out for any negative responses. Additionally, take into account infants' sensitive skin and growing respiratory systems when selecting mild oils and application techniques.

Chapter Five

Common infant ailments and essential oil solutions

Despite the increasing popularity of essential oils due to their potential health benefits, it's crucial to exercise caution when using them, especially around young children. Due to their sensitive skin and developing respiratory systems, infants may respond to essential oils differently than adults do. See a pediatrician or other certified healthcare provider before using essential oils on or around infants. Having said that, the following is a list of common infant ailments and basic safety advice for using essential oils:

- **TEETHING PAIN:** Administer a small amount of diluted chamomile or clove oil to soothe a baby's gums during teething. Once more, make sure the oil is highly diluted (less than 0.1%–1%) and keep it away from the infant's mouth and eyes.

- **CONGESTION OR COLD SYMPTOMS:** Steam inhalation is a gentle method for assisting infants with congestion. You can use a few drops in a bowl of hot water that is securely out of the baby's reach, or you can diffuse a little amount of peppermint or eucalyptus essential oil in a cool-mist humidifier in the room. Never use essential oils directly on an infant's skin or in close proximity to their face; instead, use a very low concentration.

- **COLIC OR DIGESTIVE DISCOMFORT:** Some parents find relief for their infants by gently massaging diluted fennel or chamomile essential oil on the baby's tummy. To make sure there is no negative reaction, use extremely diluted concentrations, typically less than 0.1%–1% and conduct a patch test on a little piece of the baby's skin.

- **SKIN IRRITATIONS:** People frequently use lavender essential oil due to its calming features. Apply a drop or two to minor skin irritations, such as diaper rash, after diluting it with a carrier oil, such as coconut oil. But always test on a small patch of skin first, and stop using the product right away if there are any negative side effects.

- **SLEEP ISSUES:** You can help create a peaceful and sleep-promoting environment by placing a drop of diluted lavender oil on a piece of cloth next to the baby's crib. Once more, make sure the oil is out of the baby's reach and the concentration is very low.

- **DIAPER RASH:** Use a carrier oil to gently apply

diluted lavender or tea tree oil to the affected area to relieve irritation. But always test on a small patch of skin first, and stop using the product right away if there are any negative side effects.

- **CRADLE CAP:** You can apply coconut oil directly to the scalp to soften and loosen the cradle cap, as it is both soothing and moisturizing. Apply a small amount to the scalp and massage it in gently, then wash it off with warm water.

- **FEVER:** Dilute peppermint oil in a carrier oil and apply to the bottoms of the feet to help cool the body. But, especially when dealing with young children, it's imperative to exercise caution and see a pediatrician.

- **EAR INFECTIONS:** Tea tree oil has antibacterial qualities and can be diluted in a carrier oil before applying to the outer ear. It is imperative, therefore, to speak with a pediatrician prior to applying any essential oils for ear infections.

- **GAS/INDIGESTION:** Diluting ginger oil with a carrier oil might help relieve discomfort in the digestive system. Apply a tiny quantity to the baby's abdomen and gently massage it clockwise.

Never use essential oils carelessly, especially near small children, due to their potency. It is imperative to appropriately dilute, conduct patch tests, and confer with a healthcare provider prior to administering them, particularly for newborns and young children. Furthermore, since ingesting essential oils can be dangerous, it's imperative to keep them carefully and out of children's reach.

Concluding remarks about using essential oils with infants

When using essential oils with infants, it's important to use caution and discretion, even if they can potentially help with a variety of health conditions, including those that impact babies. Here are a few things to consider:

- *Speak with a Pediatrician:* You should always seek advice from a pediatrician or other healthcare provider before using any essential oils on or near infants. They can provide advice tailored to your baby's health needs and help you make well-informed decisions about the use of essential oils.

- *Choose safe oils:* Experts believe that certain essential oils pose less risk for infants than others. In general, milder oils like chamomile and lavender are more tolerable. But since each infant is unique, you should always watch to see how your child reacts to any essential oils you use.

- **Dilution and safety:** Essential oils are potent, highly concentrated compounds that can have negative effects, particularly on infants whose skin and respiratory systems are still developing. Before using essential oils externally, always dilute them correctly in a carrier oil and use them sparingly.

- **Patch testing:** To ensure there are no negative reactions or sensitivities, test a tiny area of an infant's skin before applying any essential oil.

- **Application technique:** Exercise caution when using essential oils on infants; keep them away from delicate regions, including the face, eyes, and mucous membranes. Always apply diluted essential oils to the skin rather than directly inhaling them, especially for infants.

- *Alternative therapy:* For baby health concerns, take into account non-pharmacological therapy and alternative therapies, including warm baths, soothing music, and gentle massages.

- **Watch for negative reactions:** When using essential oils with babies, keep an eye out for bad reactions like skin irritation, breathing problems, or allergic responses. If you experience any adverse effects, stop using the product right away and get help from a doctor if needed.

- *Safe storage:* To avoid inadvertent use or misuse, keep essential oils securely stored out of children's reach.

- *Respect individual differences:* Because each baby is different, what is appropriate for one may not be appropriate for another. When utilizing essential oils or any other natural therapies, pay attention to your baby's cues and preferences.

In conclusion, medical professionals must carefully, cautiously, and supervise the application of essential oils, even though they may help with some newborn ailments. Essential oils have the potential to enhance conventional medical procedures and improve your baby's health when utilized sensibly.

ACKNOWLEDGEMENTS

All glory belongs to God. I'd also want to thank my wonderful family, partner, fans, readers, friends, and customers for their constant support and words of encouragement.